Focus On Phonics

- Suitable for differentiated work within the classroom.

- The scheme is based on multi-sensory teaching methods with the use of structured phonics and opportunities for over-learning.

- Contains worksheets to help reinforce spelling strategies as well as methods to help with the orientation of letters.

- The worksheets can be used as an assessment tool so that individual educational plans can be put into place.

- The exercises help make sequencing more automatic.

- There is additional positive reinforcement with a certificate of achievement.

Have fun!

Acknowledgements

I would like to dedicate Focus On Phonics to my father and mother Leslie and Sheila Scahill and to thank my parents for their unstinting support and love. I send my thanks and love to my children Charles and Sophie for their enthusiasm and encouragement.
I would also like to thank my friend Mary Brady for all her guidance and particularly the learning aids, which she designed for Focus On Phonics.
Many thanks to my special pal Ian Cooper for always having such confidence in me.
I would also like to thank Lonsdale Publishing for adding Focus On Phonics to their excellent portfolio.

Nicola McMullan BSc (Hons), Advanced Dip Sp LD (OCR/RSA)
Consultant: MJA Brady Cert Ed (SEN), BEd (English), MA, Advanced Dip Maths (OU), Advanced Dip Sp LD (OCR/RSA)

Contents

Notes

Introductory exercises

• Copy the letters into the spaces underneath.

Lower case

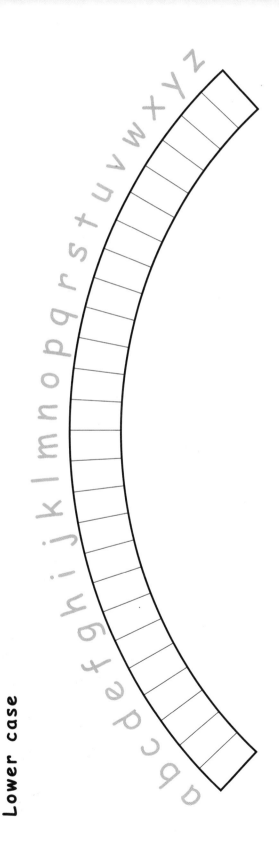

Upper case

• Join the upper case letter to the lower case letter.

Introductory exercises

- Start at the left-hand side of the page
- Keeping the pencil on the paper, circle the letter being tracked.

For example track for b

b p q d f d d q p g d p d q d b b p q g d h p j d b f d q b

Track for the following letters

b   b p a s l k q d f d d q p g d p z x c v b n m d q d b b p q d

p   p a d s f p q p n o b p q p p g d m q c b k p q d b p q g h

d   f p q b d f b p q q p g a d d e p q d m p q c h p d b b b j d

q   h d b p q c p g d a q d b e q d b n q q g j p s q e d q b p f

Now choose your own letter to track

_ _ _ p d f q p b d b p q e p g d r q d b p q k b p q f h p j d b t

Introductory exercises

• Write the letter you are tracking at the start of each row.

Track for

Introductory exercises

- Fill in the five missing letters in each arc.
- Write the completed arcs again underneath.

Lower case

a b c d e f g h * j k l m * o * q r * u v w x y z

Upper case

A B C D E F G H * J K L M * O * Q R * * U V W X Y Z

① Non-cursive and cursive script ĭ

- Practise copying the letters on the blank lines provided below.

i i i i

ℓ ℓ ℓ ℓ

Short vowel sound ĭ

- Read the word aloud.
- Cover the word, then say it.
- Write the word whilst saying it.
- Read again. Then check.

dig

lid

bin

fin

short
vowel sound

i

as in bin

pig

pin

win

tin

11

③ **Short** vowel sound ĭ

- Look at the picture.
- Say the word.
- Say the word again; listen for the short vowel sound in the middle.
- Write the missing letter.
- Copy the word again underneath.

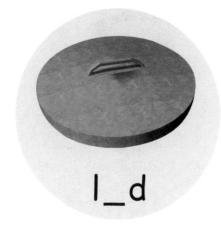

l_d

b_n

d_g

p_g

short
vowel sound

i

as in pig

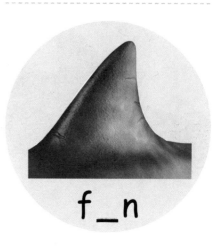

f_n

t_n

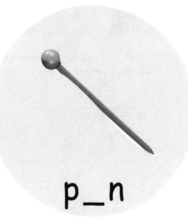

p_n

w_n

Short vowel sound ĭ

- Look at the picture.
- Say the word.
- Say the word again; listen for the initial sound.
- Write the missing letter.
- Copy the word again underneath.

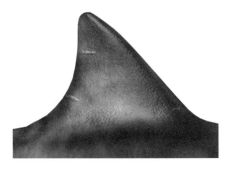

_in

_in

_id

_in

i

trace
the letter

_ig

_in

_ig

_in

⑤ **Short** vowel sound ĭ

- Look at the picture.
- Say the word.
- Say the word again; listen for the end sound.
- Write the missing letter.
- Copy the word again underneath.

di_

bi_

li_

wi_

i
trace
the letter

fi_

pi_

pi_

ti_

Short vowel sound ĭ

6

• Write the correct word under each picture.

• Now check your work.
• Look at the picture &
  read the words
  carefully.
• Check they match by
  looking at the work
  you did before.

- Join the word to the correct picture.
- One has been done for you.
- Look at the word carefully.
- Can you find more than one picture?

dig
lid
bin
fin
pig
pin
win
tin

• Track the words that rhyme with the picture.

dig   jet fig jag fin beg jog jig

lid   kid fig lad big ten leg hid

fin   bun fat bin big bat tin win

pin   web pit pat cat win peg fin

pig   peg jig jog fig hid pug hat

tin   top fat fin pop kin bin tip

- Practise copying the letters on
  the blank lines provided below.

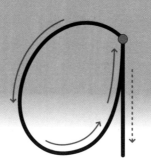

a a a a

a a a a

Short vowel sound ă

- Read the word aloud.
- Cover the word, then say the word.
- Write the word whilst saying it.
- Read again. Then check.

tap

mat

cat

bat

short
vowel sound
a
as in hat

hat

van

man

jam

19

③ **Short** vowel sound ă

- Look at the picture.
- Say the word.
- Say the word again; listen for the short vowel sound in the middle.
- Write the missing letter.
- Copy the word again underneath.

j_m

m_t

h_t

v_n

trace
the letter

b_t

m_n

t_p

c_t

Short vowel sound ă

- Look at the picture.
- Say the word.
- Say the word again; listen for the initial sound.
- Write the missing letter.
- Copy the word again underneath.

_at

_at

_at

_an

a

trace
the letter

_am

_at

_ap

_an

⑤ **Short** vowel sound ă

- Look at the picture.
- Say the word.
- Say the word again; listen for the end sound.
- Write the missing letter.
- Copy the word again underneath.

ma_

ha_

ja_

ba_

short
vowel sound

a

as in bat

va_

ta_

ma_

ca_

• Write the correct word under each picture.

• Now check your work.
• Look at the picture & read the words carefully.
• Check they match by looking at the work you did before.

7 Matching word to picture ă

- Join the word to the correct picture.
- One has been done for you.
- Look at the word carefully.
- Can you find more than one picture?

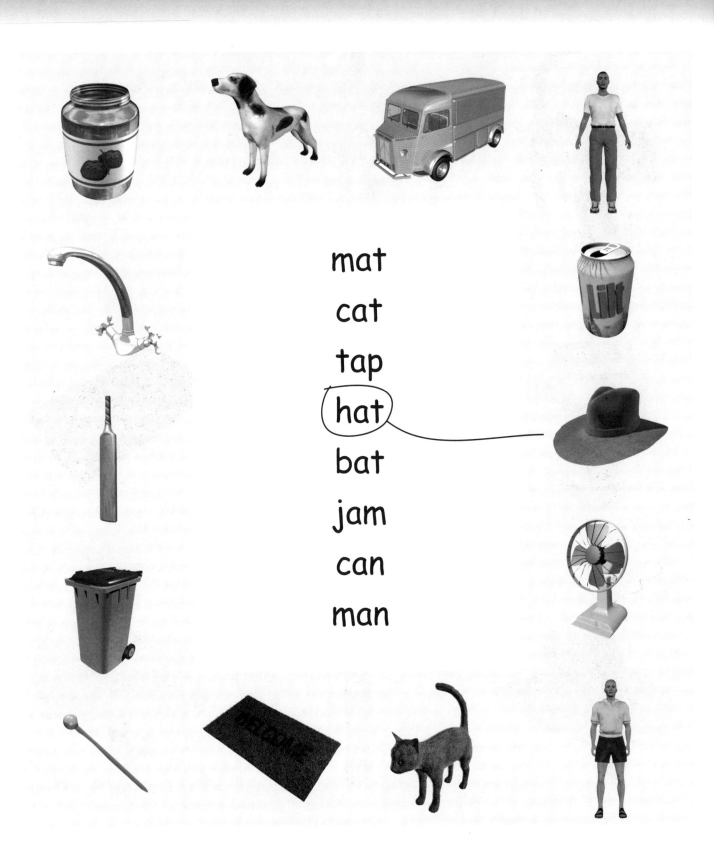

mat

cat

tap

hat

bat

jam

can

man

Track rhyming words ă

• Track the words that rhyme with each picture.

man

can fan dig ban ten mat van

hat

ham bin cat cot fat win bat

tap

tag map leg gap peg bat cap

jam

ham van hut ram vet jet fat

can

fan cap ban cot tan pup sun

fan

ham ban bug sun fat jam man

1 Non-cursive and cursive script ŭ

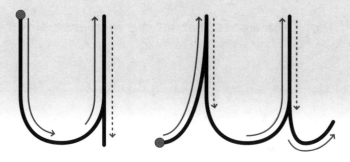

- Practise copying the letters on the blank lines provided below.

u u u u

ıı ıı ıı ıı

- Read the word aloud.
- Cover the word, then say it.
- Write the word whilst saying it.
- Read again. Then check.

hut

sun

bug

bus

short vowel sound
u
as in bus

mug

nut

bud

cup

③ **Short** vowel sound ǔ

- Look at the picture.
- Say the word.
- Say the word again; listen for the short vowel sound in the middle.
- Write the missing letter.
- Copy the word again underneath.

b_s

h_t

m_g

b_d

c_p

short vowel sound **u** as in bug

b_g

n_t

s_n

- Look at the picture.
- Say the word.
- Say the word again; listen for the initial sound.
- Write the missing letter.
- Copy the word again underneath.

_up

_ut

_us

_ud

trace
the letter

_un

_ug

_ut

_ug

5 **Short** vowel sound ŭ

- Look at the picture.
- Say the word.
- Say the word again; listen for the end sound.
- Write the missing letter.
- Copy the word again underneath.

bu_

mu_

nu_

cu_

trace
the letter

su_

bu_

hu_

bu_

- Write the correct word under each picture.

- Now check your work.
- Look at the picture & read the words carefully.
- Check they match by looking at the work you did before.

- Join the word to the correct picture.
- One has been done for you.
- Look at the word carefully.
- Can you find more than one picture?

cup

hut

bud

sun

bus

bug

cut

mug

• Track the words that rhyme with each picture.

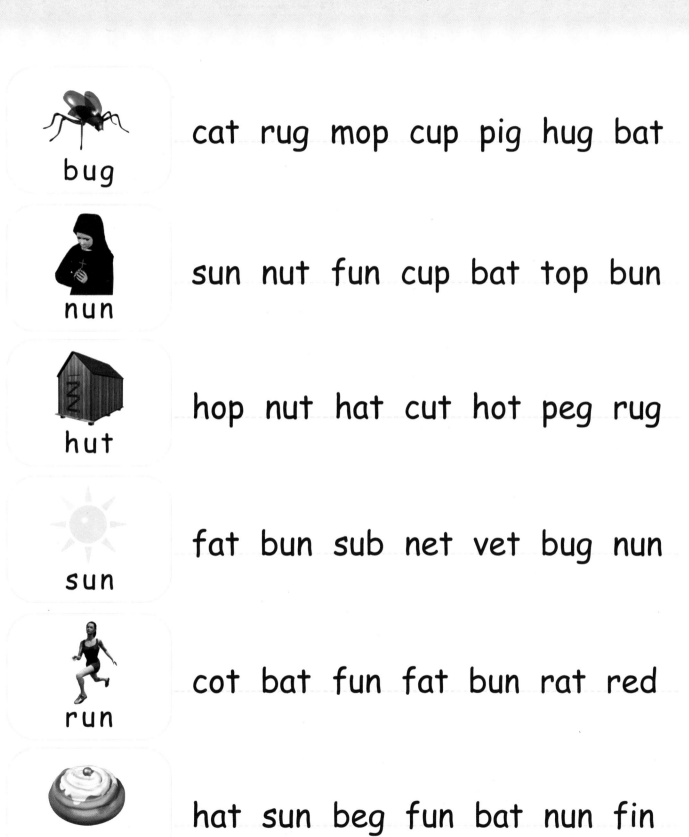

bug   cat rug mop cup pig hug bat

nun   sun nut fun cup bat top bun

hut   hop nut hat cut hot peg rug

sun   fat bun sub net vet bug nun

run   cot bat fun fat bun rat red

bun   hat sun beg fun bat nun fin

- Practise copying the letters on the blank lines provided below.

e e e e

ℓ ℓ ℓ ℓ

Short vowel sound ĕ

- Read the word aloud.
- Cover the word, then say it.
- Write the word whilst saying it.
- Read again. Then check.

bed

hen

ten

jet

short vowel sound **e** as in jet

net

beg

leg

peg

35

- Look at the picture.
- Say the word.
- Say the word again; listen for the short vowel sound in the middle.
- Write the missing letter.
- Copy the word again underneath.

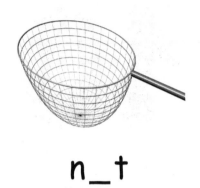

n_t

l_g

b_g

h_n

e
trace
the letter

p_g

j_t

t_n

b_d

- Look at the picture.
- Say the word.
- Say the word again; listen for the initial sound.
- Write the missing letter.
- Copy the word again underneath.

_en

_en

_eg

_eg

trace
the letter

_eg

_et

_ed

_et

⑤ Short vowel sound ĕ

- Look at the picture.
- Say the word.
- Say the word again; listen for the end sound.
- Write the missing letter.
- Copy the word again underneath.

te_

ne_

je_

be_

short
vowel sound

e

as in ten

10

be_

le_

pe_

he_

Short vowel sound ĕ

- Write the correct word under each picture.

10

- Now check your work.
- Look at the picture & read the words carefully.
- Check they match by looking at the work you did before.

7 Matching word to picture ě

- Join the word to the correct picture.
- One has been done for you.
- Look at the word carefully.
- Can you find more than one picture?

peg

leg

net

beg

jet

hen

ten

bed

• Track the words that rhyme with the picture.

peg

pup net bed jet pin dig beg

bed

dig big wed tin win lid bin

ten

pen tip men fin hen tap pip

hen

hid hat men fen kid leg bin

jet

jig cat win tin dig met bin

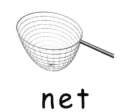
net

vet met cat bat pin jet jig

Non-cursive and cursive script ŏ

- Practise copying the letters on the blank lines provided below.

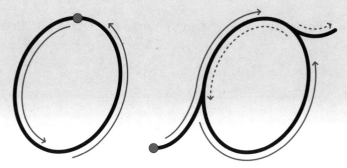

- Read the word aloud.
- Cover the word, then say it.
- Write the word whilst saying it.
- Read again. Then check.

cot

dog

mop

log

short
vowel sound
O
as in mop

pot

box

fox

rod

③ **Short** vowel sound ŏ

- Look at the picture.
- Say the word.
- Say the word again; listen for the short vowel sound in the middle.
- Write the missing letter.
- Copy the word again underneath.

d_g

m_p

l_g

c_t

short
vowel sound

o

as in box

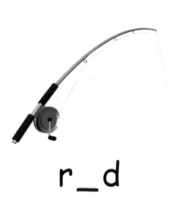

r_d

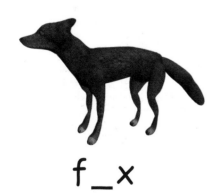

f_x

b_x

p_t

Short vowel sound ŏ

- Look at the picture.
- Say the word.
- Say the word again; listen for the initial sound.
- Write the missing letter.
- Copy the word again underneath.

_ox

_ot

_ot

_op

O
trace
the letter

_og

_og

_od

_ox

45

⑤ **Short** vowel sound ŏ

- Look at the picture.
- Say the word.
- Say the word again; listen for the end sound.
- Write the missing letter.
- Copy the word again underneath.

po_

ro_

mo_

bo_

trace
the letter

fo_

co_

lo_

do_

• Write the correct word under each picture.

• Now check your work.
• Look at the picture & read the words carefully.
• Check they match by looking at the work you did before.

- Join the word to the correct picture.
- One has been done for you.
- Look at the word carefully.
- Can you find more than one picture?

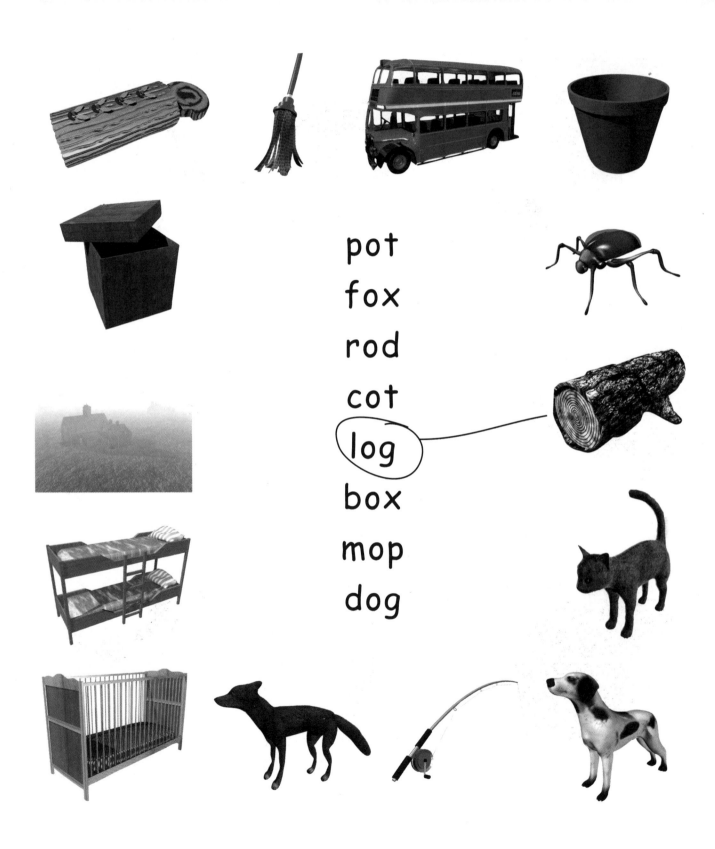

pot

fox

rod

cot

log

box

mop

dog

Track rhyming words ŏ

- Track the words that rhyme with each picture.

pot

cat pat pod cot tot top pig

fox

fan vex log bog dog box hop

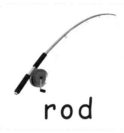
rod

rat cat cod rot bog beg red

cot

net cat cap pot can hot dog

log

lip bog leg tog bag hog fog

mop

hop pop mat pup top bog met

1 Finishing exercises

Track for words e.g. (pat)(fe)(bid)(bpig)(spig)(dmanq)(dbap)(ghap)

dmatmoppupapaqpbbatgtfrdedbatpqqgdpeq
begpupfundibphbugdenhepotupatbbedbdfunr
loghgytrdesfrboxfgtrdesdsddabtqqdbedhjuiy
tgbntapmmsunnbgfdsahamdjetnutgtrdqmetjuy
funtcupsdebusrttghpupswabugtrfsetlegpigth
djfingtrywindepintinjetfigjagjogleghjuder
fundfleghenpegcotfoxhyutgfrrodcapdeswaq

tipfrmaneghjudjibjsuabugtarfsetlegpigthdj
fingtrzwinpintinjetfigjagjrthyhrfutrgbtpuph
penpitpatcatwinpenjigjoghfunidpopbinbantan
jambtnfbnhamgdsjugugfundreswhfbrdeswerty
uiutrgbfhyuderdftcotdfredswerttotvfdcxser
thodyzedtfrdidbatpuphhrrtfgdscfdvsatdfrtew
sanetfghbinmpopbnhgytpuphubgasdfrthopbatj

mnmatbhfunicapnetbgjuytftapjasewdcfunmum
digbddjilmjagfbbpdnorsskntentapmmughf
figeplmnsbugtuibuswqapenojfxpitwnnml
mabunwebijkdrnvupodsrlbudbppafqdnpatf
aqprcupsxzhugwimetlkophotuoddbqsubwnl
netwqrratiirugnnbqpazbatfowedfawqplnm
etydmladjinikmnpugbfbrsaoqzdlogwwpqcat
fgihamqanwzbagoprddbfoxuplrodfunysrfv
awtorugrshgfatxvwdlhidjqtwfenjammkbbq

- The wizard is having trouble with his spells.
- Can you help him?
- Circle the real words coming out of his cauldron.

ben   sun   dat

pin   mat   pup

nut   bun   net   bin   dep

beb   win   fin   cat   pig   nut

ten   bed   bon   jug   jam

poq   hen

bus   hut   deg   keg

bug   dig

man

van   fud   tap

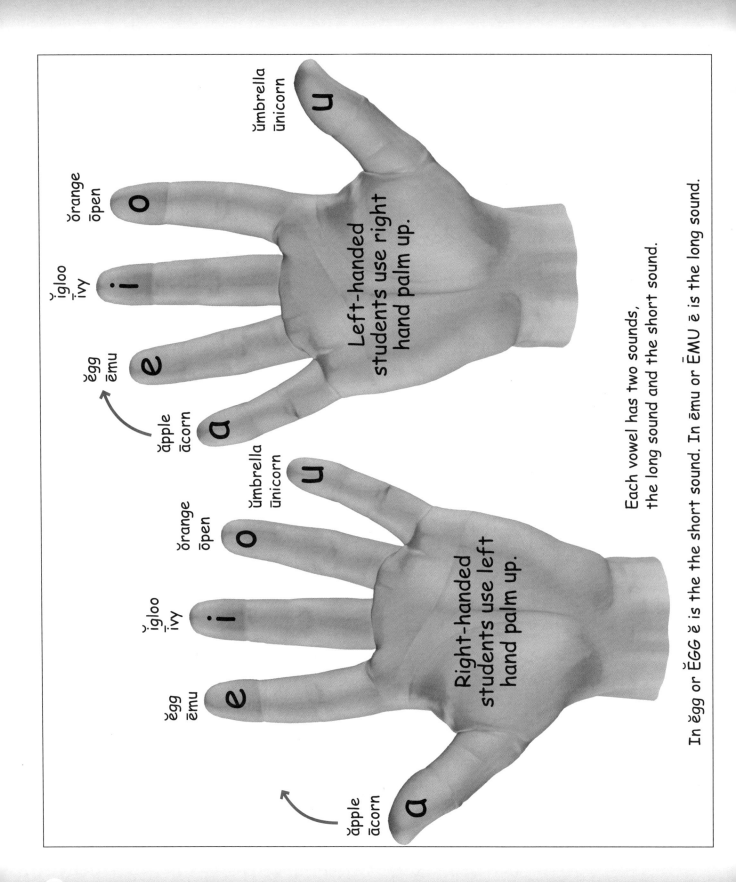

Left-handed students use right hand palm up.

ŏrange ōpen — o

ĭgloo īvy — i

ĕgg ēmu — e

ăpple ācorn — a

ŭmbrella ūnicorn — u

Right-handed students use left hand palm up.

ŏrange ōpen — o

ĭgloo īvy — i

ĕgg ēmu — e

ăpple ācorn — a

ŭmbrella ūnicorn — u

Each vowel has two sounds, the long sound and the short sound.

In ĕgg or ĔGG ĕ is the the short sound. In ēmu or ĒMU ē is the long sound.

Appendix – the letter 'b'

• Draw the bat before the ball to form the letter 'b'.

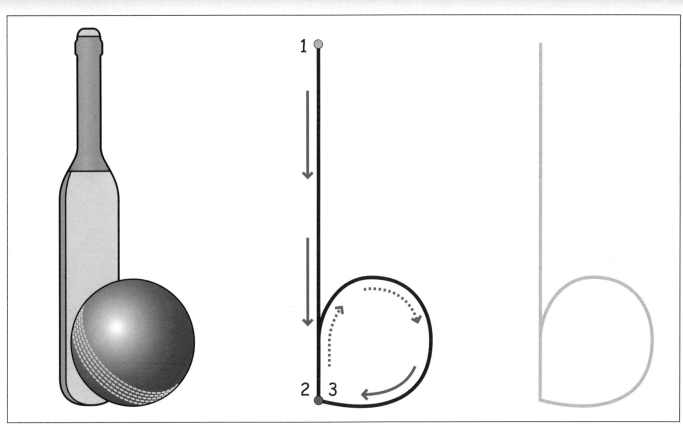

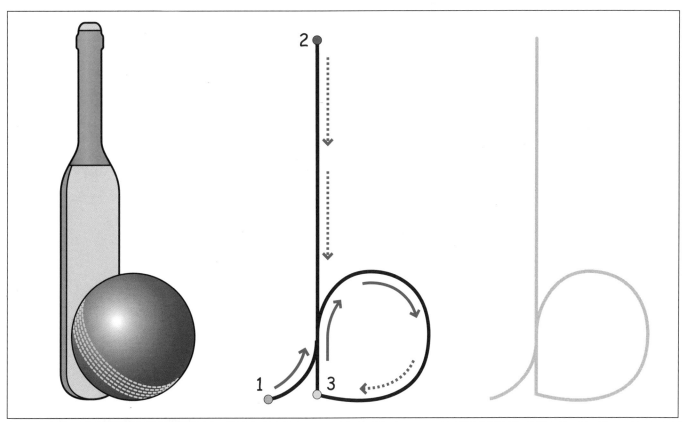

③ Appendix – the letter 'd'

- If you sometimes forget how to form the letter 'd', think of the alphabet: 'c' comes before 'd' in the alphabet so write 'c' first on your page.
- Practise this on the lines provided below.

c c c c c c c c

Once you have done that you can continue upwards with the stick of the 'd'. Practise writing the letter 'd' on the lines below.

d d d d d d d

This method will also work for cursive letters. Look at the examples below, then practise on the extra lines.

d d dd d d dd

- If you find that you sometimes get your 'b's' and 'd's' mixed up, try to remember the bed image, as shown below.

The 'b' has to come first, because the stick of the 'b' forms the beginning of the bed (headboard) and the 'd' has to come last because the stick of the 'd' forms the end of the bed.

Practise on the lines below.

play the games and reinforce what you've already learnt

There are twelve words below and twenty-four pictures on the next two pages. All the pictures need to be pasted onto cardboard, laminated and cut out.

tag   hat

bat   pan

big   hip

tip   pig

bin   fan

bag   fin

Activity 1
Place all the cards, face down, on the table. Take turns to turn over the cards. Turn any two cards face up. Do they match? Are they exactly the same picture? Are they homophones? (ie. Do they sound the same but have different pictures?). If so then you can have another go. If not, put them back in the same place. Try to remember where you put them. Continue until there are no cards left.

Activity 2
This is similar to game 1 but this time you have to decide if the last part of the word rhymes. Place all the cards, face down, on the table. Take turns to turn over the cards. Turn any two cards face up. Do they rhyme? If the pictures rhyme, then you can have another go. If the pictures do not rhyme, put them back in the same place. Try to remember where you put them. Continue until there are no cards left.

Activity 3
This is similar to game 1 but this time you have to decide if the first part of the word (the initial consonant) is the same. Place all the cards, face down, on the table. Take turns to turn over the cards. Turn any two cards face up. Do they begin with the same consonant? If the pictures begin with the same sound, then you can have another go. If the pictures do not begin with the same sound, put them back in the same place. Try to remember where you put them. Continue until there are no cards left.

Activity 4
Laminate the words and cut them out. Match each word to two pictures.

Learning aid (activity one)

- The pictures relate to the following words:
  fin; big; pig; bin; tip; hip; fan; bag; pan; bat; hat; tag.

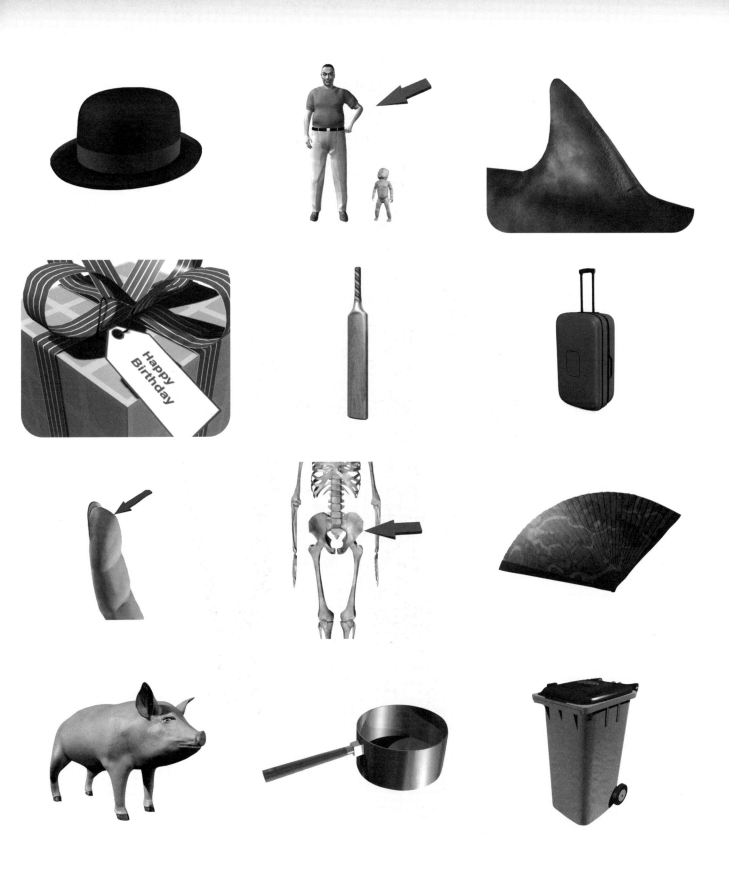

There are twelve words below and twenty-four pictures on the next two pages. All the pictures need to be pasted onto cardboard, laminated and cut out.

bed	rug
pod	bug
cog	peg
log	leg
hut	red
cut	hod

Activity 1

Place all the cards, face down, on the table. Take turns to turn over the cards.

Turn any two cards face up. Do they match? Are they exactly the same picture? Are they homophones? (ie. Do they sound the same but have different pictures?).

If so then you can have another go. If not, put them back in the same place. Try to remember where you put them. Continue until there are no cards left.

Activity 2

This is similar to game 1 but this time you have to decide if the last part of the word rhymes. Place all the cards, face down, on the table. Take turns to turn over the cards.

Turn any two cards face up. Do they rhyme? If the pictures rhyme, then you can have another go.

If the pictures do not rhyme, put them back in the same place. Try to remember where you put them. Continue until there are no cards left.

Activity 3

This is similar to game 1 but this time you have to decide if the first part of the word (the initial consonant) is the same.

Place all the cards, face down, on the table. Take turns to turn over the cards.

Turn any two cards face up. Do they begin with the same consonant?

If the pictures begin with the same sound, then you can have another go.

If the pictures do not begin with the same sound, put them back in the same place.

Try to remember where you put them. Continue until there are no cards left.

Activity 4

Laminate the words and cut them out. Match each word to two pictures

Activity 5

Add words and pictures from the previous game and then play any of the above games.

Learning aid (activity two)

- The pictures relate to the following words:
  bed; rug; pod; bug; cog; peg; log; leg; hut; red; cut; hod.

65

hat

This is to certify that

....

is a Focus on Phonics speller

signed ....

Teachers' notes

About Focus On Phonics (Book 1)

Multi-sensory teaching methods encourage the student to use as many senses as possible to retain information. They are beneficial to students of all ages and abilities, including those with general learning difficulties and specific learning difficulties (e.g. dyslexia). This book utilises multi-sensory teaching methods in a fun way and encourages self-checking in order to develop self-esteem and independence.

When worked through systematically, Focus On Phonics provides a structured phonic programme with built in 'over learning'. These additional notes are to assist teachers in adapting and tailoring the scheme to the needs of individual students.

The worksheets in this book have been designed to be clean, bright and accessible. They can be used in a variety of situations, including differentiated work within the classroom, formal assessment and remediation. For example, after the student has completed the tracking exercise on page 7, the teacher or parent could ask them to complete page 8 to assess their competence in this particular skill.

If the student is able to successfully write the correct word under each picture on page 15, then the activities on pages 57-67 can be used to help reinforce what they have learned. If the student is unable to complete page 15 successfully, then they should be encouraged to work through the background exercises from page 10 onwards.

The work sheets...

- incorporate ideas that help to teach spelling strategies
- help focus on letter orientation
- show how to form cursive script
- help upper case and lower case alphabet correspondence become more automatic

If it is thought necessary to formally mark the student's work, this should be in the form of a tick in a colour of the student's choice – there should be no crosses. If the student makes an error it should be discussed, but the teacher should not write on the student's work.

Access to this scheme should be based on ability, not age. The teacher or parent should encourage the student to start working at a level where they feel comfortable and then encourage them to progress carefully and systematically through the scheme to build on and develop their knowledge. Activities have been provided (pages 57-67) to help reinforce student learning. They have been designed so that peers and siblings can play an active role in this process. Teachers' notes suggest how the activities could be adapted to increase their difficulty as the student progresses through the scheme.

Focus On Phonics can benefit students of any age. References to key stages and spelling ages have been deliberately omitted. When students need extra reinforcement they may feel embarrassed if they think they are being given work that is aimed at a younger age group.

Explore, learn and enjoy.

Please note, it is important that specialist help is sought if a student continues to experience difficulties.

Teachers' notes

Introductory exercises

Page 5
Alphabet arc – upper and lower case: Before this page is attempted, it would be beneficial for the student to be given complete sets of lower and upper case letters (e.g. wooden, plastic or magnetic) to arrange into separate arcs. This activity could be timed. To help focus the student's attention, ask them to close their eyes whilst you wrongly orientate or remove a letter. This can be extended to include several letters. Let the student repeat the exercise for you to attempt!

Page 6
Matching lower case and upper case letters: A variety of fonts have been introduced to make this exercise slightly harder. To extend and reinforce what is being taught, provide a selection of letters in different fonts for the student to match.

Page 7
Tracking letters – b, p, d, q: It is important that the student tracks from left to right and keeps the pen on the paper. The final box has been left blank so that you, or the student, can choose the final letter to be tracked. If a student is transposing letters, please see Appendix (pages 53-55) for strategies to help with remediation. Continue to reinforce correct orientation and note any difficulties.

Page 8
Tracking letters – unspecified: Use this worksheet to continue reinforcing correct orientation.

Page 9
Alphabet arc – missing letters: Encourage the student to use the letters they have identified to make words (e.g. pints / PINTS). Focus on the rhymes: *in, ip, is,* and *it*. Having used the remaining letters, ask the student to select a certain number of consonants from the arc and to make as many words as they can. This activity can be repeated, focusing on the onsets: *pi, ni, ti, si*. Use the step technique to extend this.

Short vowel sounds

Pages 10, 18, 26, 34, 42
Practice pages – non-cursive and cursive script: For these pages, the student should be encouraged to use a highlighter or a pen with an italic nib, as this will help with the formation of the letters and the flow of their writing.

Pages 11-15
Teaching pages (ĭ): As an extension to these exercises, and if it is appropriate, the student could be given letters (e.g. wooden, plastic or magnetic) and asked to create the words.

Page 16
Matching words to pictures (ĭ): The additional pictures on this page have been selected and included to necessitate careful reading.

Page 17
Tracking rhyming words (ĭ): This exercise requires careful concentration, as the student needs to retain more than one piece of information to complete it successfully.

Teachers' notes

Pages 19-23
Teaching pages (ă): As an extension to these exercises, and if it is appropriate, the student could be given letters (e.g. wooden, plastic or magnetic) and asked to create the words.

Page 24
Matching words to pictures (ă): The additional pictures on this page have been selected and included to necessitate careful reading.

Page 25
Tracking rhyming words (ă): This exercise requires careful concentration, as the student needs to retain more than one piece of information to complete it successfully.

Pages 27-31
Teaching pages (ŭ): As an extension to these exercises, and if it is appropriate, the student could be given letters (e.g. wooden, plastic or magnetic) and asked to create the words.

Page 32
Matching words to pictures (ŭ): The additional pictures on this page have been selected and included to necessitate careful reading.

Page 33
Tracking rhyming words (ŭ): This exercise requires careful concentration, as the student needs to retain more than one piece of information to complete it successfully.

Pages 35-39
Teaching pages (ĕ): As an extension to these exercises, and if it is appropriate, the student could be given letters (e.g. wooden, plastic or magnetic) and asked to create the words.

Page 40
Matching words to pictures (ĕ): The additional pictures on this page have been selected and included to necessitate careful reading.

Page 41
Tracking rhyming words (ĕ): This exercise requires careful concentration, as the student needs to retain more than one piece of information to complete it successfully.

Pages 43-47
Teaching pages (ŏ): As an extension to these exercises, and if it is appropriate, the student could be given letters (e.g. wooden, plastic or magnetic) and asked to create the words.

Page 48
Matching words to pictures (ŏ): The additional pictures on this page have been selected and included to necessitate careful reading.

Page 49
Tracking rhyming words (ŏ): This exercise requires careful concentration, as the student needs to retain more than one piece of information to complete it successfully.

Teachers' notes

Finishing exercises

Page 50
Tracking for words: The student is tracking for words that contain the short vowel sounds. It is important that they track from left to right and keep the pen on the paper. If a student is transposing letters, please see the Appendix (pages 52-55) for strategies to help with remediation. Continue to reinforce correct orientation and note any difficulties.

Page 51
Identifying words: The student needs to examine each word and decide if it is real. By this stage, they should be able to distinguish nonsense words. As an extension, and if appropriate, the student could be encouraged to write the words on a separate piece of paper or use a word processor (link with IT skills) and arrange them in alphabetical order.

Appendix

Page 52
Teaching strategy – the vowels: If right handed, the student will start with their left thumb and use their right hand to indicate. If left handed, the student will start with their right little finger and use their left hand to indicate.

Page 53
Teaching strategy – the letter 'b': This is to reinforce the correct letter formation. Encourage the student to use a highlighter or a pen with an italic nib. As the student writes the letter they should voice 'bat before ball' (this can be
done mentally).

Divide a piece of paper into four sections:
• Section 1 - write the letter for the student to trace.
• Section 2 - the student writes the letter.
• Section 3 - fold the page so that the student writes the letter from memory.
• Section 4 - the student writes the letter with their eyes closed.

Page 54
Teaching strategy – the letter 'd': This is to reinforce the correct letter formation.

Page 55
Teaching strategy – the letters 'b' and 'd': This is to reinforce the correct letter formation and help the student distinguish between 'b' and 'd'.

Learning aids

Pages 57-67
Activities 1 and 2: Instructions and notes about these activities can be found on the respective pages.

Certificate

A certificate has been included to provide positive recognition of the student's achievement in successfully completing Focus On Phonics (Book 1).